Sam and His Doll

by Katrina Davino • illustrated by Nadja Sarell

Lucy Calkins and Michael Rae-Grant, Series Editors

LETTER-SOUND CORRESPONDENCES

m, t, a, n, s, ss, p, i, d, g, o, c, k, ck, r, u, h, b, e, f, ff, l, ll, j

HIGH-FREQUENCY WORDS

is, see, the, no, has, his, too, of, says, go, to, for, look, me, he

Sam and His Doll
Author: Katrina Davino
Series Editors: Lucy Calkins and Michael Rae-Grant

Heinemann
145 Maplewood Avenue, Suite 300
Portsmouth, NH 03801
www.heinemann.com

Copyright © 2023 Heinemann and The Reading and Writing Project Network, LLC

All rights reserved, including but not limited to the right to reproduce this book, or portions thereof, in any form or by any means whatsoever, without written permission from the publisher. For information on permission for reproductions or subsidiary rights licensing, please contact Heinemann at permissions@heinemann.com. Heinemann's authors have devoted their entire careers to developing the unique content in their works, and their written expression is protected by copyright law. We respectfully ask that you do not adapt, reuse, or copy anything on third-party (whether for-profit or not-for-profit) lesson-sharing websites.
—Heinemann Publishers

"Dedicated to Teachers" is a trademark of Greenwood Publishing Group, LLC.

Cataloging-in-Publication data is on file with the Library of Congress.

ISBN-13: 978-0-325-13816-9

Design and Production: Dinardo Design LLC, Carole Berg, and Rebecca Anderson

Editors: Anna Cockerille and Jennifer McKenna

Illustrations: Nadja Sarell

Photographs: p. 32 © Sergey Nivens/Shutterstock; inside back cover (jet) © Philip Pilosian/Shutterstock; inside back cover (jam) © pogonici/Shutterstock.

Manufacturing: Gerard Clancy

Printed in Dongguan, China
4 5 6 7 8 9 10 TP 28 27 26 25 24 23
April 2023 Printing / PO# 4500868396

Contents

1 Sam's Doll 1

2 Pancakes for Dinner 13

3 Sam Is Up 23

Sam's Doll

Sam looks at his doll.
"Let's dress up!" he says.

Sam jogs to his bed and gets a bin.

The bin has lots of dress up stuff!

Sam gets a bib for his doll…

and a red cap.

Sam digs in the bin.

He gets 1 sock, 2 socks.

The socks go on the doll.

Sam digs and digs in the bin.

The doll gets pants and clogs and mitts.

Sam gets a big sun hat and looks at his doll.
The doll has a hat.
Can it get 2 hats?

It can!

Sam jams the sun hat on his doll.

Sam picks up his doll.

"OK!" he says.

"Let's go get dinner!"

Pancakes for Dinner

It is Mom!

Sam gets his doll.
Dad gets the dinner,
and Mom gets a rest.

"Pancakes for dinner?"
Sam asks.
"Pancakes for dinner!"
Dad says.

"Can I add a bit of jam?"

Sam asks.

Dad nods.

Sam adds a LOT of jam.
A big blob of it!

Sam dips his pancakes in the jam.

Sam dips his doll in the jam too!

The doll has a LOT of jam on it.

Dad gets a rag and dabs at it.
Sam dabs at it too.

Did Sam get the jam off?
He did!

Sam Is Up

Sam sees a big, bad bug.

It nips and snaps and...

Dad jogs in. Mom jogs in.
"Sam?" Mom asks.

Sam sits up and hugs his doll.

He sobs.

"A big, bad bug! It ran at me!"

It is a job for Mom and Dad!

Mom and Dad tuck Sam and his doll in.

Mom hums.

Dad rubs Sam's back.

A kiss, a hug, and back to bed.

Learn about...

DREAMS

Whoa! Is that talking puppy real? No, it's just a dream. People have dreams about all kinds of things—silly things, scary things, sad things, happy things. But why do we have dreams?

No one knows for sure why we dream, but scientists have some ideas. One idea is that dreams help your brain create memories. *Memories* are things that you remember for a long time. If you didn't have dreams, you would forget a lot of what you learned that day.

Another idea is that dreams help people to be creative. Many artists, writers, musicians, and inventors say they get their best ideas from their dreams. For example, Larry Page, one of the founders of the company Google, says he got the idea for Google from a dream! Have you ever gotten an idea from one of your dreams?

Talk about...

Ask your reader some questions like...

- What happened in this book?
- How did jam get all over Sam's doll?
- How did Sam's parents help him feel better after his bad dream?
- Sam loves to play dress-up with his doll. What do you love to play?